LEARNING TO HEAR GOD'S VOICE

THE HOLY SPIRIT SERIES: STUDY 2

LEARNING TO HEAR GOD'S VOICE

A 4-Week Study Guide

Matt Reynolds, Maggie Ulmer, and Emma Winchester

Copyright © 2025 by Spirit and Truth

All rights reserved. No part of this publication may be reproduced, stored in a retrieval system, or transmitted, in any form or by any means—electronic, mechanical, photocopying, recording, or otherwise—without prior written permission, except for brief quotations in critical reviews or articles.

Scripture quotations, unless otherwise indicated, are from the Holy Bible, New International Version®, NIV®. Copyright © 1973, 1978, 1984, 2011 by Biblica, Inc.™ Used by permission. All rights reserved worldwide.

ISBN: 978-1-966666-01-1

Spirit and Truth
P.O. Box 954
Tipp City, OH 45371

Printed in the United States of America.

Contents

Series Overview	vii
How to Use This Study	ix
Introduction	1
Week 1: Does God Really Want to Speak to Me?	3
Week 2: The Different Ways God Speaks	15
Week 3: Whose Voice Am I Hearing?	29
Week 4: I Think I Heard from God, Now What?	41
Conclusion	53

The Holy Spirit Series

This series of study guides will introduce the person and work of the Holy Spirit. Christians were never intended to live on their own strength or serve God solely by their own effort. In the Old Testament, the Holy Spirit is active in creation and given to specific people (like prophets) at specific times and for specific purposes. Starting with Pentecost, God has poured out his Spirit upon all believers, bringing salvation, transformation, gifts, miracles, and so much more. The Christian life that Jesus invites us into is impossible apart from God's indwelling presence. This series is designed to help you get to know the third person of the Trinity in a more intimate and active way. The Christian life you always wanted, and the life our hurting world needs, requires us to live in greater obedience to the Holy Spirit. We hope these back-to-the-basics study guides will be tools that help you discover in greater measure the fully-alive way of living that Jesus died to give you.

How to Use This Study

This study guide can be used in groups or by individuals. You can take the four chapters at your own pace, but it is designed to be used as a weekly guide. Each chapter contains three sections: Read, Reflect, and Respond.

READ

Each chapter starts with a scripture reading. Take some time to quiet yourself before the Lord. Say a brief prayer asking the Lord to illuminate his Word by his Spirit. Then read the passage once or twice to yourself. After you have spent some time in the chapter's scripture, continue by reading the short chapter. If using this in a small group, the "Read" section can be used in two ways: If time allows, consider reading the scripture and chapter as a group. Another option is to have everyone read the scripture and chapter before coming to your gathering.

REFLECT

Next, take some time to reflect on the reading using the reflection questions. If you are doing this study on your own, it may be helpful to write down your answers in a journal. Writing out a response can help bring clarity and insight. If you are using this study in a group, use the reflection questions to guide your discussion together on the chapter's content. Be as vulnerable as you can be as you respond. Powerful learning occurs when believers are transparent with one another.

RESPOND

The "Respond" section is your weekly action step. This is a chance to put into practice something related to the chapter's content. Don't skip this part! Learning about the Holy Spirit is not merely a mental exercise. The Holy Spirit is personal, and fully understanding him requires experiencing him. If you are doing this study on your own, we recommend that you journal about your experience on the "Respond" prompt. If you are using this study in a group, the action step is your challenge in-between meetings. Begin the upcoming week's meeting by discussing your experience from the previous week's action step.

Introduction

It's quite a statement to say, "God speaks to me." And yet that is a claim Christians have held true since the beginning of our movement. The pages of the Bible, from beginning to end, are full of stories of God communicating with his people. From the very start humans were made to be a people who walk and talk with God. Intimacy in any relationship requires communication and God desires intimacy with us. We serve a God who speaks! The question is, "Are we listening?"

There are many ways that God chooses to reveal himself and his will to us. In this study we will examine some of those ways and how to listen for God's voice more intentionally. Whether through the pages of Scripture, the nudges of the Holy Spirit, or the witness of Godly community, the Christian life is fundamentally about learning to hear what God is saying and discerning how to respond. And just like anything in life, the more we practice, the better we get. Learning to hear God's voice is essential if we want to live in everyday obedience to his will. So, let's jump in and begin this study with faith that God still speaks to his people...and that includes you!

WEEK 1
Does God Really Want to Speak to Me?

READ: Psalm 95

God Speaks!

Christians believe that God speaks. This may not seem like a radical statement. However, the Christian conviction that our God communicates with humanity has important implications for how we understand God's nature and mission. Saying that God speaks means there is an intended audience: us! Furthermore, as God's intended audience, he has made a way for us to hear him. It also means he has things he wants to tell us. God is communicative and interactive. He intervenes in time and history, and he desires for human beings to know him.

We'll discuss in later chapters the ways God speaks. If you survey the entire Bible, there are countless accounts of God speaking. God speaks through creation. He speaks audibly to Adam and Eve. The Lord reveals himself in physical manifestations like he did in the burning bush, or the pillar of cloud and fire in Exodus. God also speaks through visions to Paul, or through dreams as he did to Joseph. Throughout Acts God the Holy Spirit speaks to the Church. The pinnacle of God's communication is in Jesus Christ, in whom God, who is spirit, takes on the likeness of a human being so he can communicate with his creation.

Why Does God Speak?

Why would God want to speak to us? From page one of scripture, we see that God has a plan to make a family and a home where he and that family dwell together. Scripture tells us over and over of God's desire to be with human beings. Variations of the phrase "I will be their God, and they will be my people" appear multiple times throughout the Bible, with the first version of it occurring in Genesis 17:7 when God tells Abraham he will establish a covenant with him, his children, and subsequent generations of children. But even before Abraham came Adam and Eve. They were God's first human children with whom he spoke and spent time in the Garden of Eden.

The reason God desires to be with us is simple. He loves us, and he has made us to be with him, love him, and worship him. When God made Adam and Eve they were without sin, immortal, and lived in perfect union with

God. Conversation at this level of intimacy flows easily. However, when Adam and Eve rebelled, the flow of easy intimacy between human beings and the Father was severed. Since that moment, the Father has pursued humanity to restore his original design and intention for creation. Restoring communication with us is an important part of God's redemptive plan.

Communication between God and human beings, specifically those who become his children through the new birth, is part of God's design and order for creation. In Romans 1:20, Paul says, "For since the creation of the world God's invisible qualities—his eternal power and divine nature—have been clearly seen, being understood from what has been made, so that people are without excuse." Here, Paul is talking about God's way of communicating his presence through creation to those who do not know him yet. This passage demonstrates God's desire to reveal himself to us so that we have the opportunity to experience conviction for our sins, repent, and be saved.

No doubt most of us have read or heard the well-known scripture verses from the gospel of John: "For God so loved the world that he gave his one and only Son, that whoever believes in him shall not perish but have eternal life. For God did not send his Son into the world to condemn the world, but to save the world through him" (3:16-17). This is the heart of the gospel. God's desire is to make a people for himself. He intends to restore the broken bonds of relationship lost in the Garden. He knows that this is not something we can accomplish on our own, so he made a way for us through Christ. Through the Holy Spirit, we can grow in our sensitivity to his voice. God is a patient teacher. Learning the ways God communicates and how to recognize his voice takes time and practice.

Barriers to Hearing God's Voice

We know that the conversational exchange between God and human beings doesn't always go smoothly. From the beginning, human beings have faltered in the practice of listening and obeying the leading of the Father's voice. Take a moment and read through Genesis 3. Consider that the state of original sin that all human beings are born into is the result of Adam and Eve not obeying the authority and goodness of God's words. Sin entered the world when humans stopped listening and obeying what God was speaking to them.

There can be many reasons we may struggle to hear God. As Paul points out in 1 Corinthians 13:12 "Now we see only a reflection as in a mirror; [one day] we shall see face to face. Now I know in part; then I shall know fully, even as I am fully known." Meaning, there are many mysteries that prevent us from fully knowing and understanding God and we won't have answers to those mysteries until we are with him in the afterlife. Other things that prevent us from hearing God clearly are more mundane and human, like sin.

Psalm 95 describes an internal state of the heart called "hard-heartedness." Even those who have decided to follow Jesus can become hard-hearted. In Scripture, hard-heartedness often describes a lack of sensitivity and responsiveness to God's words and voice. Hard-heartedness can be caused by many things: lack of faith, unforgiveness, ignorance of the doctrines and traditions of Christianity, and unrepentant sin, just to name a few.

When we are hard-hearted we fail to grasp what is of ultimate importance, and how desperately God desires us to be a listening people. In Matthew 23:37, Jesus lamented the impending judgment and ruin of Jerusalem. He cried out: "Jerusalem, Jerusalem, you who kill the prophets and stone those sent to you, how often I have longed to gather your children together, as a hen gathers her chicks under her wings, and you were not willing." This verse comes at the end of what is sometimes called the seven woes to the Pharisees and teachers of the Law. The judgment that fell upon the leaders of Jerusalem was because they did not recognize Jesus for who he is. God was speaking and they did not listen. The God to whom they had devoted their life's work stood before them in the flesh, and yet they were unable to grasp his true identity.

If we are going to avoid the sin that led to rebellion in the Garden, and ignorance among the Pharisees, we must learn to hear and discern what God is saying. Listening for God's voice and responding in obedience is a central feature of the Christian life.

The story of young Samuel in 1 Samuel 3 is an example of this principle. Samuel lived in the temple at Shiloh worshipping in the presence of God. He first heard the voice of the Lord as a child however he did not recognize the voice as belonging to God. Samuel sought guidance from the High Priest of the temple, Eli. Eli was able to provide wisdom and instruction for Samuel. Eli realized that the Lord was going to continue speaking to Samuel so he taught him a listening prayer:

> Eli realized that the Lord was calling the boy. So Eli told Samuel, "Go and lie down, and if he calls you, say, 'Speak, Lord, for your servant is listening.'" So Samuel went and lay down in his place. The Lord came and stood there, calling as at the other times, "Samuel! Samuel!" Then Samuel said, "Speak, for your servant is listening." (1 Sam. 3:8-10)

We, too, must learn to live as people to whom God speaks and pray the words that Eli taught Samuel: "Speak, Lord, your servant is listening."

A Posture of Faith

God speaks to his children for many reasons. As a loving Father, he wants to communicate with his children. He speaks to correct us, teach us, give us wisdom, encourage us, and express his love towards us. He also speaks in response to our questions and needs. God can give insight into the most mundane circumstances if we are open to his counsel.

Consider the story of Abigail, the wife of Nabal. Abigail acted with wisdom after Nabal offended future King

David by refusing to help him and his men while they were on the run from King Saul. Abigail's humility saved her husband's life and the lives of her household servants when she apologized for her husband's inhospitable behavior. Sensing God's hand at work in David's life, she accurately prophesied that David would reign successfully in the future as King over Judah, and would one day unify and reign over all of Israel. David gave credit to God for Abigail's faithfulness and insight. He praised God for sending her to speak with him: "David said to Abigail, 'Praise be to the Lord, the God of Israel, who has sent you today to meet me.'"

What if Abigail had thrown her hands up in exasperation and defeat? Abigail's posture of faith made all the difference in her interaction with David. She lived with a belief that God could and would guide her actions and words. Abigail became an instrument of God's will. When we live open to God, we will be blessed by receiving his presence and communication and we get the privilege and thrill of being his messengers!

Psalm 139:1-4 describes in detail the Father's intimate knowledge of his children:

> You have searched me, Lord,
> and you know me.
> You know when I sit and when I rise;
> you perceive my thoughts from afar.
> You discern my going out and my lying down;
> you are familiar with all my ways.

> Before a word is on my tongue
> you, Lord, know it completely.

The psalmist goes on to say there is no place we can go where God's presence cannot reach us. God created our innermost being, and his thoughts for us outnumber the grains of sand! "How precious to me are your thoughts, God! How vast is the sum of them..." God allows us to know him. He intends for his children to know his thoughts. It is his pleasure to tell us.

The Christian approach to knowledge and understanding is different from the world's approach. We believers begin with the belief that what God says about himself is true. We allow faith in partnership with reason, and the Holy Spirit, to draw us into a deeper revelation of who God is, and how he does things. This idea is called "faith seeking understanding." The phrase was coined by a 12th-century monk named Anselm of Canterbury. But the notion of our faith being the proving ground of what we know about God goes all the way back to Jesus himself: "Blessed are those who believe without seeing (John 20:29)."

It's perfectly understandable to struggle with the idea that God speaks and that we are made to hear his voice. It's especially difficult if we don't feel like we have experiences of hearing him. Later chapters will explore the ways God speaks and how to discern his voice. But first, we begin from a place of faith that what scripture says about God is true, including the reality that God can and does speak to us. We take into serious consideration the warning that rejecting God's voice can lead us to hard-heartedness.

Fortunately, the antidote to unbelief is simple, although it's not always easy. All we must do is confess our trust in God and take a step of faith wherever we previously resisted him. So today, if you struggle to believe that God speaks, that he wants to speak to you, or if you are afraid you won't be able to perceive God communicating with you, do not harden your heart in unbelief! God speaks, and because you are his child, he wants to speak with you! He wants to share his perspective on your circumstances. He wants to give you guidance about when to act and when to wait on him. He wants to lead you to people around you who need his words of love and encouragement. He created you to hear his voice so that you can be a partner in his mission to redeem the world. Hearing God's voice begins with faith. God still speaks to his children. He wants to speak to you personally.

REFLECT:

1. What is your favorite story from scripture that describes God speaking, and why?

2. Can you think of a moment in your own life when you thought you discerned God "speaking" to you?

3. Are there any areas of unbelief you have identified in your understanding of how and why God wants to communicate with you? Make a short confession and repent of them now. Know with confidence that, in the name of Jesus Christ, you are forgiven!

4. Is there any way scripture describes God communicating with human beings that you would like to experience?

RESPOND:

For this week's action step, take your answer from question 4 and write a prayer. Begin the prayer with, "God, I have faith, and believe that you want to speak to me...." Then be bold to ask the Lord to speak to you in the way you identified. End your prayer with, "Speak, Lord, your servant is listening." Testify to a trusted friend or your small group about any responses you hear from God.

WEEK 2
The Different Ways God Speaks

READ: 1 Kings 19:9-18

Humans are made to communicate because we were created in the image of a God who loves to speak. We see him communicate directly with Adam and Eve in the beginning. That was his original design–for us to walk and talk with our Creator. At the end of the Bible we read John's vision of the new creation. In this coming reality, God and his people are in perfect relationship for all eternity. This relationship involves humanity worshiping God and God speaking back to his children. The Bible is a story of God speaking to people and people speaking back to God.

That does not mean that God always speaks in the same ways. The Bible records God communicating in a myriad of ways. Try to recall some of the different modes of communication as you think over the stories you know in the Bible.

- God speaks audibly (1 Samuel 3).
- God speaks through angels and messengers (Luke 1:26-38).
- God speaks through dreams (Genesis 37:1-11).
- God speaks through visions (Acts 10:1-23).
- God speaks through circumstances (Jonah 1-2).
- God speaks through ordinary people filled with the Holy Spirit (Acts 2).
- God speaks through the discernment of community (Acts 15:1-35).
- God speaks through specially called representatives, like prophets (see Isaiah, Jeremiah, etc.).
- God speaks through creation and even animals (Romans 1:20, Numbers 22:21-39).
- God speaks through music (see the Psalms).
- God speaks through his inspired Word (2 Timothy 3:16).
- God speaks through his Son, who came to earth in the flesh (Hebrews 1:1-2).
- God speaks through the Holy Spirit, who was poured out on all flesh at Pentecost (Acts 2).

God uses a variety of means to draw his children closer to him.

Why does God use so many different means to speak? Think about all the different relationships you have in your life. If you are a parent and have multiple children, it's likely you have learned that you have to communicate with each of them somewhat differently. Or think of the friendships you have; each person receives communication differently. When you love someone, you try to communicate in a way they can best understand. God knows us better than any human because he made us. So he chooses unique ways to communicate with each of his children. It's all an act of grace!

There is another reason that God's voice comes through in various ways. His primary desire is to have a relationship with you, not simply to give you information. God chooses to communicate in ways that are intimate, require faith, and cause us to lean in closer to Him.

This week's Scripture reading centers on Elijah and his encounter with God at Mount Horeb. A powerful wind sweeps over the mountain, but God is not in the wind. An earthquake comes, but the Lord does not speak through the earthquake. Next is fire, but God's voice is not in it. Finally, Elijah hears a gentle whisper. God speaks in a still, small voice.

Why? Notice what Elijah does. He hides in a cave during all the commotion. But when things calm down and he hears the whisper, verse 13 says he goes out and stands at the mouth of the cave to listen. God speaks in ways that lead us to closer proximity to him. Consider when a loved one whispers something in your ear. What is the automatic response to hear that small voice? You lean in. A whisper is an act of intimacy. It causes you to draw close to the one who is speaking.

God shows so much love by speaking in the ways he does. God's primary heart is not about relaying information or giving you instructions. He wants you. He wants you to know him. He wants you to understand his heart. He wants you to walk in faith and trust him. His goal is intimacy. And he communicates accordingly by the grace of his sovereign wisdom.

Hearing God's Voice is Normal for Christians

Hearing God's voice is not strange. For New Testament believers, it is supposed to be normal and frequent. How do we know that? The book of Acts gives us a snapshot into the life of early believers. What you find are disciples of Jesus who are directed by his voice through the Holy Spirit.

There are many short phrases in Acts that we easily gloss over because they sound too familiar to us. For example, in Acts 13, the Holy Spirit speaks to the church gathered at Antioch, and in turn, they send Barnabas and Saul off on a mission. Verse 4 reads, "The two of them, sent on their way by the Holy Spirit..." In Acts 16, we read about Paul and his traveling companions, and verse 6 says, "having been kept by the Holy Spirit from preaching the word in the province of Asia." These are just two examples where the Spirit directs people in very practical ways on what to do and where to go.

What does that mean practically? It means that early believers learned to hear God's voice clearly enough, through the indwelling Holy Spirit, that their physical plans were directed or redirected according to his communication. They changed travel and ministry plans by the Holy Spirit's leading.

When we read Paul's letters to various churches, like 1 and 2 Corinthians, we see that the Holy Spirit was not only speaking to the Apostles but was speaking in miraculous ways to ordinary believers scattered throughout the world in churches that worshipped Jesus Christ. And none of this has stopped since Biblical times. Church history is full of countless examples of God still speaking to his children. Clearly, God still wants to speak to believers today.

So, how does God speak? And how can we learn to intentionally listen?

As noted above, there is no one set way that the Holy Spirit speaks to people. God can communicate through anything! He is God after all. However, there are some basic ways we can learn to hear him more clearly. There are some ways revealed in the Bible and demonstrated throughout Christian history that are predictable ways to hear God's voice.

Scripture

The first place to begin hearing God is through the Bible. New Testament writers clearly reflect the belief that God speaks through Scripture by constantly quoting verses from the Old Testament. The New Testament, as we know it now, was canonized by the end of the 4th Century, though the writings of the Gospels and letters were used in the church long before that. For hundreds of years, Christians all over the globe have believed and taught that God speaks through the Scriptures.

Paul writes to Timothy:

> But as for you, continue in what you have learned and have become convinced of, because you know those from whom you learned it, and how from infancy you have known the Holy Scriptures, which are able to make you wise for salvation through faith in Christ Jesus. All Scripture is God-breathed and is useful for teaching, rebuking, correcting and training in righteousness, so that the servant of God may be thoroughly equipped for every good work. (2 Timothy 3:14-16)

Paul says that the Scriptures are "able to make you wise for salvation." That means God uses the Bible to show us how to be saved.

He also says that "all Scripture is God-breathed and is useful for teaching, rebuking, correcting and training in righteousness..." Think about how God created Adam in Genesis. He gave Adam a form, a human body, but it was not until he breathed into his nostrils that he really came to life. Or think about the famous prophecy about dry bones in Ezekiel 37. The bones are assembled and flesh is put on them, but it is only when the wind of God, his breath, comes into them that the army comes to life. Finally, think about Pentecost. When the Spirit falls, the first experience of his presence is described as wind. God breathes, and the church is born.

Scripture reveals that God's breath is essential for something to come to life. When Paul says that all Scripture is God-breathed, he means that the Bible is more than mere words on a page. It is not simply history or literature. It is alive and active; it has the breath of God in it. And as we read the Word, we can discover real life.

If we want to hear God's voice, we must begin by reading scripture with a desire to hear from God, not simply to learn information about God. You might even try a simple prayer as you read the Bible this week, such as: "Lord, I am here and I want to hear from you. Would you make your Word come alive for me as I read? I don't want to just know about you, I want to know you. Speak, Lord, for your servant is listening."

God is never silent in our lives if we are intentional to read his Word.

Prayer

When you pray, do you take time to listen? We often say that prayer is a conversation with God, but no true conversation only includes one person. That is a speech, not a conversation. As Christians, it can be easy for us to slip into the habit of telling God all the things we need or want without ever giving him a chance to speak.

Prayer is the intentional act of turning our attention to God and allowing our hearts and minds to be in a place of communion with him. Sometimes this includes talking, whether out loud or quietly in our minds, but this should also include silence and extended times of listening.

When we listen in prayer, what are we listening for? God can use all sorts of things to speak to us, and our main job is to pay attention. As you sit in silence and give God space to speak, you may notice a variety of things. At first, it may seem hard to silence your own thoughts. We live in a busy world, and we all have things swirling around in our minds: to-do lists, anxieties, family issues, etc. Allow yourself a good amount of time to allow all of that to calm down. You don't have to fight these thoughts; just intentionally surrender them to the Lord. As things come into your mind, you might simply say, "God, I give this to you."

After a while, you may find yourself in a place where there is less noise in your thought life. Then try asking God a simple question. "Lord, is there something you want to say to me today?" In the next chapter, we are going to talk more about discerning God's voice and how you know if you are hearing the Holy Spirit. For now, just pay attention to whatever comes to mind and try to discern if it might be from God.

Does a scripture, a song, an image, a random thought, or an internal impression come to mind? Pay attention. You might even want to write it down. When listening in prayer, a journal of some kind can be helpful to document what you hear.

Learning to hear God's voice through prayer is like any other spiritual discipline. The more you try, the more comfortable it will become. Just like reading Scripture gets more natural with time, so does listening prayer.

Nudges Throughout the Day

In addition to dedicated times of prayer, we also want to learn to hear God's voice in everyday activities. Ultimately, we are seeking a life as Christians where our overall posture is constant listening and trying to respond in obedience.

Have you ever had a thought repeatedly come to your mind to the point that you think maybe God is trying to get your attention? He probably is. Have you ever had a friend or family member keep coming to mind in a way that seems random? God may be trying to lead you to prayer or nudge you to call them.

Listening to God's voice on a daily basis requires us to take these nudges seriously. We always want to use good discernment. Ask yourself: Does what I am hearing align with Scripture? Does this seem to be in line with what I know about God's character? Does this seem like something that will produce good fruit, like the fruit of the Spirit (Galatians 5:22-23) in me or someone else? If the answer to these quick mental discernment tests is yes, then just try it. Attempted obedience is never wasted with God, no matter what the outcome of that step of faith may be.

Community

Finally, hearing God's voice often happens in community. We need the spiritual wisdom of brothers and sisters to help us know what God is saying, and he often chooses to speak to us through others. This might come in a simple word of encouragement, a moment of accountability, or through a prophetic word. Intentionally surrounding ourselves with spiritual family is one of the most important practices that can help us hear God's voice with frequency and clarity.

We see this truth demonstrated in the Scriptures that describe the New Testament church. Certainly, we hear from God in our private times and quiet places. However, we often hear from God through other Christians. If you want to hear God's voice and discern more clearly how he is speaking to you, put yourself in proximity to other believers who also believe God speaks.

Conclusion

God is not silent. He speaks to his children. He wants a relationship with us, and relationships always involve communication. Look at the Garden of Eden before the fall; God spoke openly to Adam and Eve. This is his heart for his creation. Sin often causes us to close our ears to him, but that does not change God's desire and heart. Through the gift of the Holy Spirit, he makes his presence and voice available to all flesh. God so desires to speak to you, he has taken up residence within you! Jesus died so that he could make a way for this restoration of relationship and full communication. So let's not take that for granted! There is nothing better than learning to intentionally listen and realizing that the God who created all things is communicating with you personally. Listening and responding in obedience is at the heart of Christian living.

REFLECT:

1. As you read the list at the beginning of this chapter on different ways God speaks, can you think of moments when God spoke to you in some of those ways? Name some of the instances where you felt you were hearing from God. What were the circumstances involved? How did you discern it was God's voice?

2. How is reading Scripture to hear God's voice different than reading to gain more information? Both are good, but it can be tempting to do only one or the other. Which feels more comfortable for you? How could you adjust your posture of reading to prioritize hearing God's voice and moving closer to him?

3. Have you ever tried listening prayer? If so, what was the experience like? What did you find difficult? What did you hear?

4. What are some ways that God speaks that seem foreign to you?

RESPOND:

This week, pick a specific time and place to try listening prayer. Get a journal or something with which to write. Go back and read the section on hearing through prayer in this chapter. Follow the basic instructions and sit with God for at least 15 minutes in silence. Write down anything you think might be God speaking to you.

WEEK 3
Whose Voice Am I Hearing?

READ: 1 Corinthians 13:4-8

Learning the Character of the Good Shepherd's Voice

In the opening verses of John 10, Jesus tells the Pharisees that the sheep of the Good Shepherd know his voice and will not follow anyone else. There is an important principle in Jesus' words: the sheep have learned the character of their Shepherd's voice, and are not easily led astray by competing voices. As followers of Jesus, our work is to become experts in God's voice and have a healthy awareness of other voices.

In 1 Corinthians 13:4-8, Paul writes these famous words:

> Love is patient, love is kind. It does not envy, it does not boast, it is not proud. It does not dishonor others, it is not self-seeking, it is not easily angered, it keeps no record of wrongs. Love does not delight in evil but rejoices with the truth. It always protects, always trusts, always hopes, always perseveres. Love never fails.

God's voice will never contradict his character. His character is revealed through the witness of his son Jesus Christ, the revelation of himself through the words of scripture, and through the witness of the Holy Spirit. When Paul wrote the famous words above to the Church at Corinth, he was writing about the greatest gift imparted from the Holy Spirit to believers, the gift of holy love. This love surpasses human love and perfectly reflects the character of the Trinity. Everything God communicates to human beings is rooted in his perfect love. As an exercise, read the passage above three times, each time replacing the word "love" first with Father, then Son, and finally with Holy Spirit.

Because God desires to speak into every part of our lives, not everything that we hear from God may sound explicitly like a message of affection or love. In John 14:26, Jesus tells the disciples that the Holy Spirit will guide them and remind them of everything they have already learned. In John 16:8-10, Jesus says the Holy Spirit will convict people of their sin and their righteousness. We also know from 1 Corinthians 12 that the Holy Spirit gives and communicates through spiritual gifts meant to build up and edify the body of Christ. From these handful of passages, we can know that God will speak to us to:

- Guide us into wisdom.
- Teach us about his truth.
- Remind us of things he has said before.
- Convict us of sin.
- Give us assurance of our righteousness in Christ.
- Reveal his glory through spiritual gifts.

These various messages and types of speech flow from God's primary attribute: love. In addition to being love, God is also truth. As such, he cannot lie, contradict himself, or go back on any promise. Take a moment to read the following passages about the faithfulness of God's Word and character:

- Numbers 29:13 (God cannot lie.)
- Psalm 19:7 (God's teachings make us wise.)
- Proverbs 33:4 (God's word is a protective shield.)
- Isaiah 55:11 (God's word always accomplishes its purposes.)
- Matthew 24:35 (God's word is eternal.)
- Luke 21:15 (God will give us his words to speak in our time of need.)
- Hebrews 6:13 (God's promises are certain.)
- 2 Timothy 2:13 (God remains faithful.)

Considering the Source of What We Hear

Just as God's voice sounds like something specific, and does specific things, there are also things that God will never say or do. Remembering the list from above. If we begin from a place of believing that God cannot lie, contradict himself, or break his promises, then it follows that things we hear that seem to contradict these truths should be evaluated for their credibility. When discerning the root source of what we hear in prayer, in our thoughts, or even things other people say to us about God, there are three possible options: God, the Enemy, or the human self. We have already discussed the nature of God's voice, but it is helpful to know what the other two sound like to help with our discernment.

The Voice of the Human Self

How do we know the difference between our human thoughts and God's voice at work in our lives? First, we know that God is entirely different from human beings. Even though Jesus Christ was fully human, he was also fully God. The co-occurrence of his divinity with his humanity means that he is unique. This expressed itself through his sinless nature. Because of this, Jesus' actions and words are inherently challenging to our fallen human impulses. Jesus calls the weak blessed and the poor rich. We must be dependent if we want to walk in the authority of our inheritance in the Kingdom of God.

Things that we hear in prayer, impulses that pop into our minds, or challenges issued from friends that lead us into greater sacrifice, faithfulness, and holy discomfort are likely from God. If you suddenly have an impulse to share the Gospel with a coworker who does not even know that you are a Christian, it is likely that idea didn't come from you. The secondary impulse that usually follows, that doesn't want you to do anything awkward or risk being labeled as a religious fanatic, is likely the human response. Words that affirm our desires for comfort, or desires for uninterrupted accomplishment of our personal plans are almost always from us. God is not interested primarily in our comfort. He is interested in making us holy by drawing us into closer proximity to him. Learning to discern the difference between his voice and ours often reveals his holiness and, by contrast, our need to grow in holiness.

Perhaps you're wondering if our thoughts and God's thoughts are always at odds. They certainly can be. When we become a new creation through new birth in Christ, and by the process of sanctification, we can develop increasing measures of sensitivity to God's voice and desires. The alignment of our inner narrative and thought-life with God's values and truth is an important sign of our sanctification. In Romans 12:2, Paul writes, "Do not conform to the pattern of this world, but be transformed by the renewing of your mind. Then you will be able to test and approve what God's will is—his good, pleasing and perfect will". 1 Corinthians 2:16 says, "Who has known the mind of the Lord so as to instruct him? But we have been given the mind of Christ." Can you believe it? We have been given the mind of Christ! We can learn to surrender our minds to the Holy Spirit. We do this by "taking every thought captive"(2 Corinthians 10:5) and by meditating on "things above, not on earthly things" (Colossians 3:2). One of the fruits of the Christian life is that our thoughts will increasingly become the thoughts of Christ!

The Voice of the Enemy

As children of God, there is no reason or need to live in anxiety or fear of Satan. Christ came to destroy the works of the Devil, and he completed that work through his death, resurrection, and ascension. This means, until the final judgment, that the Enemy's domain has been significantly limited. The Enemy's authority exists in degrees of access that we give through our sin. Furthermore, in any discussion relating to Satan and his authority, we must remember that his authority is not, nor has it ever been, equal to God's authority. Satan is a creature. He is not eternal as God is eternal. God has no beginning or end; he is the beginning and the end. Satan has a beginning, and he will most certainly have an end.

An important way that believers can guard against the temptations and attacks of the enemy is to know the difference between God's truth and the enemy's lies. In John 10:10, Jesus tells us, "The thief comes only to steal and kill and destroy; I have come that they may have life and have it to the full." When Jesus says "steal and kill and destroy," he is speaking of the manner in which Satan tempts and deceives believers away from saving faith in Jesus Christ.

A common tactic of the enemy is to exploit areas of pain and insecurity in our lives by tempting us to indulge in our fears and inflaming our sense of shame over past sins, failures, and shortcomings. The voice of the enemy can lead us into fatalistic thinking. Fatalism is a way of thinking and believing that says all outcomes are predetermined and there is no opportunity for reconciliation, redemption, or salvation. Fatalism is the path to condemnation. This is not God's way. God does not want to condemn us for our sins. He died for us while we were still sinners so that we could be saved! God will lead us through the process of feeling convicted for our sins. This is meant to lead us to confession, repentance, and restoration to God through his forgiveness toward us.

The enemy wants us to believe that our anxious, fearful, or self-doubting thoughts are normal and right. The enemy will utilize worry as a way of tempting us to depend on ourselves rather than God. He will say we should fear uncertain outcomes because he knows it will lure us to grasp for control rather than surrendering our lives into God's hands. He will accuse us with self-doubt and self-loathing until we are emotionally and spiritually exhausted and give in to self-justification through work, and being needed by other people. This is one of his primary tactics. The enemy knows that if we are deceived about God's grace, he can lead us away from God.

We use the same strategy to shut down the voice of the enemy that we do to discipline our own voice. First, we take words, thoughts, and conversations captive and evaluate their credibility against what God says. Because the enemy's primary target is us, knowing what God says about us provides us with truth to combat the enemy's lies. The following verses give us a picture of how God sees us:

- Luke 10:17, 19 (We have authority over the enemy.)
- John 5:24 (We have everlasting life.)
- John 8:31-33 (We are set free.)
- Romans 8:17 (We are more than conquerors.)
- 1 Corinthians 5:21 (We are the righteousness of Christ.)
- 1 Corinthians 6:19 (We are the temple for the Holy Spirit.)
- Ephesians 1:4 (We are holy and without blame before God.)
- Ephesians 6:10 (We are strong in Jesus.)
- Colossians 2:10 (We are complete in Christ.)
- 1 Peter 1:23 (We are God's children.)
- 1 John 5:18 (We are born of God, and the evil one has no right to us.)

Conclusion

Learning to hear God takes time and is something we will practice throughout the entirety of our earthly lives. Seeking his voice doesn't mean we will always hear it, and even when we hear it, we won't always understand or interpret him correctly. But we can learn to discern between the different voices we hear. We can grow to discern what is from God, what may be from the Enemy and what are our own self-oriented thoughts. Studying the loving and holy character and voice of God in scripture helps us do this. Proverbs 25:2 says "It is the glory of God to conceal a matter, but it is the glory of Kings to search a matter out." Seeking out the treasure of God's voice is part of how God glorifies and sanctifies us.

REFLECT:

1. Have you ever thought about the possibility of three different sources for the things you hear in your mind? Having learned that framework, what are some ways you personally feel like you have heard each of those voices?

2. Have you ever practiced taking your thoughts captive? What was that experience like? Did you discover something about yourself?

3. Have you ever heard something critical and unkind in prayer and believed it was God speaking to you? Have you ever heard something loving in prayer and rejected it because it seemed too good to be true?

4. Does understanding God's nature, and how he sees you, change how you see yourself?

RESPOND:

This week, during your prayer time, read Psalm 139. When you are finished, visualize yourself on a long, expansive stretch of sandy shoreline next to water. With verses 17 and 18 in mind, visualize yourself scooping up a handful of sand. Allow the sand to fall through your fingers until one grain remains. This grain of sand represents one of the Father's precious thoughts for you. Ask him in prayer to tell you what it is. Don't edit what you hear, simply discern according to what you know about how God sees you. Write down anything the Holy Spirit may say or show to you. Do this exercise anytime you wish to meditate on the Father's thoughts for you.

WEEK 4
I Think I Heard from God, Now What?

READ: John 10:1-18 and John 15:1-11

So far, this study has covered God's intention for his children to hear his voice, the different ways God speaks to his children, and how to discern between the voices we may hear. The next natural question to ask is, what do we do when we hear God's voice? The answer to that question is both simple and complicated. In John 10, Jesus declares that he is the Good Shepherd, and his followers are his sheep. He tells his disciples and the Pharisees that his sheep know his voice, and when he calls to them, they follow. Jesus' sheep recognize and follow his voice. These are two distinguishing factors of being followers of Jesus

Christ. As his sheep, we should know what his voice sounds like and how to follow him when we hear his voice calling to us. This Scripture reveals the simple answer: when we hear the voice of God, our response is obedience.

The term "obedience" is what makes the answer to this question complicated. There is not one "right" or "correct" response of obedience to God's voice, primarily because it depends on what he says! So, what do we do when we hear something from God? We keep listening! This is the moment when discernment matters most. We cannot assume that everything we hear is to be shared, posted, or proclaimed from a street corner! We also cannot shrink back and withhold what we hear when God has asked us to partner with him by sharing his thoughts with someone else. We have to continue to seek wisdom about how to steward what we hear.

When we hear God speak to us, we should ask him a few questions:

- Who is this for (myself, another person, a group of people)?
- Why are you speaking to me about this?
- Do you want me to share what I have heard with anyone?
- Is there an action I am called to take in response?
- Is what you have spoken a word for right now or for the future? In other words, should I respond immediately or at a later moment?

When God Speaks to Us About Us

Most of what we hear from the Holy Spirit will be for us and about us. This is because the Holy Spirit's primary work is to sanctify us individually. He leads us closer to Jesus and makes us more like him. Jesus is described in Scripture as loving, just, compassionate, gentle, strong, humble, slow to anger, kind, gracious, merciful, and faithful. We can all admit that we fall short in these characteristics. Jesus is perfectly loving, perfectly just, perfectly compassionate, and so on. We are not. We need the help of the Holy Spirit to become more like Jesus. The Holy Spirit will speak to us about our spiritual fruit, areas of pruning, things that need to be surrendered, our habits, our lifestyles, our word choices, our time, our stewardship, and more. He talks to us about our own lives in order to make us more like Jesus. We respond to his voice by repenting, surrendering, obeying, and allowing him to form us.

Jesus teaches this principle in John 15. While speaking to his disciples, Jesus shares a word of encouragement by using the imagery of a vine, a vinedresser, and the vines' branches. Jesus says that the vinedresser is God the Father, the true vine is God the Son, and we are the branches. Immediately, Jesus gives insight into the Father's values. In John 15:2, he says, "He cuts off every branch in me that bears no fruit, while every branch that does bear fruit he prunes so that it will be even more fruitful." Did you catch it? The Father is looking for good fruit. A primary value of the Kingdom of God is fruitfulness. Jesus continues with the image and says that a branch cannot bear fruit on its own, but only when it is connected to the vine. So, "abide in me," he says. It is only when we abide in Him, and he in us, that we bear any fruit. In other words, we can only be like him if we spend time with him and allow him to change us from the inside out.

In John: 16-17 Jesus spoke a promise that he would send one after him who would be with us forever, dwelling with us and in us. At salvation, we receive an infilling of the Holy Spirit, who abides with us and in us. We become a temple for him. The Holy Spirit speaks to us in order to sanctify us and connect us back to Jesus. When we partner with what the Spirit speaks to us, we will bear fruit. This is fruit that the Father loves because it is like his Son.

The bottom line is this: the Holy Spirit helps us stay connected to Jesus and he will most frequently speak to us about ways we can grow in Christlikeness. God is always pruning us for more growth! When we hear God's instructions and nudges, our job is to always say "yes" by taking small steps of obedience each day. For example, the Spirit may speak to us about harboring unforgiveness. Rather than ignoring this internal nudge, we turn to prayer and say, "Holy Spirit, thank you for revealing this to me. Lord, help me to forgive this person. I want to forgive like you have forgiven me."

It is important to add that every believer has received the infilling of the Holy Spirit at salvation. A great way to discern what God is speaking to us is by sharing what we hear with other Spirit-filled believers. We were not made to do life alone. We were not made to keep God's voice to ourselves! We were made to discern God's voice and direction in the context of the Church, God's people. Every believer should seek relationships in the Church where they can discern God's voice and leading together. By listening to God's voice for ourselves and one another, our discernment becomes sharper. The whole body is built up and edified when we discern God's voice together.

When God Speaks to Us About Others

What we've just described is how to respond to God's voice when he speaks to us about ourselves. But what do we do when God talks to us about other people, places, or situations? Let's start with the Biblical basis for this concept. All throughout Scripture, God uses people as his messengers to speak to others. Think of the prophets. God called them to speak to various people and nations on his behalf. They shared messages that warned God's people of coming judgment if they continued to rebel. They also shared messages of hope and restoration because of God's faithfulness. Consider Isaiah, Jeremiah, or Ezekiel. God gave them very specific words to proclaim to the nations. God spoke to them, and they shared what they heard.

In the New Testament, we know that Jesus was led by the Holy Spirit. (See Mark 1:12 for example.) We read examples where Jesus offered supernatural insight like with the Samaritan woman at the well. In John 4, Jesus interacts with this lost and burdened woman. The turning point in their interaction was when Jesus shared a divine insight that could not be known by human wisdom: She had five husbands, and the man she was with now was not her husband. This opened up a spiritual conversation between Jesus and the woman. Because of this interaction, the woman believed that Jesus was the Messiah. Jesus, filled with the Holy Spirit, shared a piece of information that he divinely knew, and the woman came to faith. Additionally, the whole town heard about Jesus because of the woman's testimony. Jesus shared a divine word and many lives were changed.

God still speaks to us about other people, places, or situations. And we are called to be good stewards of what God shares with us. Oftentimes, God will speak to us about other people and situations simply because he is asking us to intercede for them. He will often speak to us about others in order that we more specifically align our prayers with his. Hebrews 7:25 tells us that Jesus lives to make intercession for us. That's right! Jesus is praying for us! When the Holy Spirit shares something with us about another person, we should respond with gratitude. God has just invited us into the sacred work of intercession. We can align our prayers with Jesus' prayers for others. Remember what John 15 taught us? When his word abides in us, we can ask anything in his name and it will be done. When we hear something from the Holy Spirit, we can agree with his will and ask for it to be done.

Sometimes, the Holy Spirit speaks to us about other people, places, or situations in order that we might share what we heard with others! Sharing what we hear from the Holy Spirit can inspire faith, reveal God's love, and draw others closer to God. Proverbs 18:21 says, "The tongue has the power of life and death, and those who love it will eat its fruit." As Spirit-filled believers, God has given us the ability to speak life and share God's love with other people. Once again, we should be filled with gratitude for this reality. God desires to use us as vessels for spreading his love and life with others.

Let's go over a few practical guidelines for sharing with another person what we may have heard from God:

1. **Pray before you speak.** As mentioned previously, it is imperative that, before we share with others out of ambition or conviction, we pray for wisdom on what to share and how to share it.
2. **Ask these discernment questions about the word you plan to share.** Does it give glory to Jesus Christ? Is it consistent with Scripture? Will this word lead the person closer to Jesus? Do I have a personal bias that is shaping this word?
3. **Qualify everything.** We suggest that you "qualify" what you have heard with language like "In prayer, I sensed God saying..." or "As I was praying for you, I felt like God was showing me..." or "The other day when I was praying, I experienced God's love for you and wanted to encourage you by saying..." These qualifying terms help to communicate that we are imperfect messengers. When we share something we hear with another person, we should approach the conversation

humbly. Sometimes we hear incorrectly. Sometimes we communicate imperfectly. Sometimes something that feels very strong to us is not actually as urgent as it seems. By reminding the person that what we share is something we sensed or felt, as opposed to "thus saith the Lord," we give the person more freedom to discern.

4. **Encourage further discernment.** In the same way that the person sharing has a responsibility to discern and steward what he or she has heard, the person receiving has a responsibility to discern and steward what he or she has received. Paul tells us in 1 Thessalonians to "test everything, and hold fast to what is good." A good principle when you share something from the Holy Spirit is to encourage the other person to pray and discern for themselves about the word.

5. **Share the truth in love.** Finally, embody Godly love and compassion as you partner with the Holy Spirit. The words we say, the way we say them, and the fruit of our lives are important in how we obey God's voice. Remember that God most often speaks to us about ourselves. Anytime we get to share God's voice with others is a privilege and a weighty responsibility. Pray for God's character to be made manifest in you as you partner with him.

Ultimately, we are all individually responsible for stewarding what we hear God speaking to us. If he is speaking to us personally, we are responsible for obeying him. This may look like repentance, surrender, increased spiritual disciplines, and/or forgiveness. If he is speaking to us about others, we are responsible for obeying him. This may look like God inviting you to intercede for the person or situation, or to share with them what you have heard. The foundation of this entire chapter is this: we must discern and obey. To discern, we must abide and ask Jesus more questions before acting hastily. To obey, we have to take actual steps, whether those are steps of intercession, personal action, or sharing with others. Like John 10 showed us, Jesus is calling to his sheep. We, as his sheep, are called to listen to his voice and follow in obedience.

REFLECT:

1. How have you responded when God has spoken to you in the past? Are there times when you knew you were responding in obedience? Have there been times when you knew you were ignoring God's voice?

2. Is there any specific area of your life where you feel like God has been speaking to you recently?

3. Have you ever experienced someone else sharing a word with you that they sensed God gave them for you? What was it like to receive a word from someone else? How did you discern if this was from the Lord?

4. Have you ever had the experience of God speaking to you about other people or situations? What was that like? How did you respond?

RESPOND:

This week's response is twofold. First, prayerfully ask the Holy Spirit to speak to you individually. You may pray what David prayed: "Search me, God, and know my heart; test me and know my anxious thoughts. See if there is any offensive way in me, and lead me in the way everlasting" (Psalm 139:23-24). Allow the Holy Spirit to show you areas of your life that may need to be surrendered, sins from which you may need to repent, or fruit that needs to be pruned. Respond by yielding yourself to Jesus, however he may lead you. Notice David's final prayer, "Lead me in the way everlasting." Ask the Holy Spirit to show you your next faithful step of obedience.

Second, ask the Holy Spirit to bring to mind one person who needs an encouraging word. Maybe an old friend or coworker comes to mind. Once he has brought someone to mind, spend a few minutes praying for that person. You may pray for blessing, health, their circumstances, or even for them to be drawn closer to God. After praying for them, ask the Holy Spirit to give you an encouraging word that you could share with them. It may be as simple as, "God sees you," or "God really loves and cares for you." Spend time listening to the Holy Spirit's voice, and remember the discernment questions we discussed earlier in the chapter. Then, call or text the person you were praying for and share with them what you heard!

Conclusion

This study guide started with the basic question, "Does God really want to speak to me?" Through this study, we hope that you have discovered in a fresh way that God indeed still speaks and that wants to speak to you personally.

There is much more that could be said on this topic, but the most important thing is for us to practice intentionally listening for God's voice. The more we listen, the more we hear.

If you started a new practice of listening prayer or reading scripture in a new way, keep going! There is tremendous fruit that comes from learning to live in a constant posture of openness to God's voice. All that God desires for our lives (encouragement, identity, healing, boldness in ministry, and more) comes in greater measure as we lean in to listen and then exercise the muscles of surrender and obedience.

Let us continue to live with the prayer of Samuel always on our lips, "Speak, Lord, your servant is listening."

AMEN

Spirit & Truth

At Spirit & Truth we long to see the church fully alive! We exist to help equip a global movement of local churches to become empowered by the Spirit, rooted in the truth, and mobilized for the mission.

Our ministry comes out of the Wesleyan/Methodist family of churches and works to bring renewal to local congregations, networks, and denominations. We offer hands-on equipping for local churches, regional conferences, online resources, podcasts, and more.

To learn more, go to **spiritandtruth.life**.

Made in United States
Cleveland, OH
02 September 2025